Testimo

Its Importance, Place and Potential

Mark J Cartledge

Chaplain and Tutor, St John's College, Durham

GROVE BOOKS LIMITED
RIDLEY HALL RD CAMBRIDGE CB3 9HU

Contents

The Cover Illustration is by Peter Ashton

First Impression July 2002
ISSN 1470-8531
ISBN 1 85174 504 1

Introduction[1]

We all tell each other stories. In fact some of us are rather good at it!

Sometimes the contexts of these stories are formal, for example as witnesses in the law court or the public enquiry. Most of the time we tell each other our stories in informal ways. Directions to the nearest bus stop might well be interweaved with our personal story of bus journeys—perhaps to the annoyance of the person who asked! We rely significantly upon the testimony of others regarding everyday matters. We do this unless we have good reason to question their stories in some way. In the Gospel of John, we read that the Samaritans believed in Jesus because of the testimony of the woman who encountered Jesus at the well. She testified that Jesus had told her everything she had ever done (John 4.39)! This motivated the Samaritans to find out more from Jesus themselves. Later in the gospel, we read that the work of the Holy Spirit will be to testify to Jesus once he has left the disciples (John 15.26). The disciples are also called to testify since they have been with Jesus from the beginning (John 15.27). Testimony, therefore, has an important role to play within Christian discipleship and the church's mission.

The word 'spirituality' is used commonly today and is something of a slippery term. From a Christian perspective it concerns the spiritual life of faith which contains devotional practices and concrete behaviour. Alister McGrath defines Christian spirituality in the following way:

> Christian spirituality concerns the quest for a fulfilled and authentic Christian existence, involving the bringing together of the fundamental ideas of Christianity and the whole experience of living on the basis of and within the scope of the Christian faith.[2]

The process can be seen to comprise a search for the God who is revealed in Christ and an encounter with this same God through the Holy Spirit, which consequently effects change or transformation.[3] Testimonies within charismatic spirituality are usually located within a narrative structure. People tell of their need and desire for God and his kingdom, how God has met and continues to meet them in their search and changes their lives in conformity with his purposes of salvation.

The aim of this booklet, therefore, is to explore the notion of testimony within charismatic spirituality. I shall draw upon recent pentecostal scholarship, philosophy and biblical theology before applying an understanding of testimony to a case study from the Toronto Airport Christian Fellowship. After which I shall suggest theological and practical guidelines, and make suggestions for the use of the liturgical tradition of the Church of England.

2

Testimony and Knowledge

Sources of Knowledge

Contemporary philosophers are beginning to appreciate what the Christian church has known for a long time—that testimony is an important source of knowledge. It is therefore interesting to observe that, in his recent work *Epistemology*, the philosopher Robert Audi outlines five sources for knowledge of ourselves and the world around us. Although Audi does not argue for a theological understanding of these sources, I suggest that they can be readily transposed into theology.

The first source is *perception*; through our fives senses we perceive the world around us. The reality of the external world is mediated to us by means of our senses. If one's senses are open to the world around, then that world is perceived and one tends to form beliefs about it. These perceptions are indeed fallible, but nevertheless real.

The second source is *memory*. Memory does not produce beliefs but it preserves what is known. It is often a basic source of the justification of belief. For example, we might remember our experience of conversion or 'Baptism in the Spirit' and use that memory to explain such a belief to others.

The third source is our inner perception or *consciousness*. 'When we look into our own consciousness, we find beliefs also arising in the same natural, seemingly irresistible way in which they arise from outer perception. We have, however, far more control over the scenes and events that we experience only inwardly.'[4] The inner and outer world both produce beliefs that are direct and irresistible.

The fourth source is *reason*. Reason enables us to turn our attention to abstract matters while being bombarded by sensory information. It enables us to makes inferences from information known to us and extends our use of categories and relations. It enables us to cohere what we sense, remember and imagine into a framework.

The fifth source is *testimony*. There is so much that we cannot possibly know without relying on others. Beliefs and knowledge are significantly grounded in social reality. This social dimension is often informal, through casual conversations, but also through literature and the media, now including the internet.

Audi summarizes these sources and how they function in terms of knowledge when he says:

> Perception looks outward, and through it we see the physical world. Memory looks backward, and through it we see the past, or at least some of our own past. Introspection looks inward, and through it we see the stream of our own consciousness. Reason looks beyond experience of the world of space and time, and through it we see concepts and their relations. Testimony draws on all these sources. It enables others to see—though at one remove, through the attester's eyes— virtually anything that an accurate and credible person attests to.[5]

Thus the individual aspects of knowing are integrated socially by the notion of testimony. It is the social mechanism of testimony that is of supreme importance to pentecostal and charismatic understanding of our knowledge of God. We do not believe and know God in isolation; rather, we are part of a worshipping and witnessing community of faith.

These features can be integrated within the theological structures by prioritizing the testimony of Scripture above other aspects. The Bible as the book of the church, read within the covenant of faith, provides a unique testimony to the purposes of God for the salvation of his creation. As Scripture is read and expounded within the community of the church, so God's testimony through the writings of his servants is heard. It constantly refreshes the corporate memory of individual congregations and gives a strong basis for hope of future blessings. There is a positive correlation between the biblical accounts and the realities to which they testify. However,

> 'for pentecostals ...belief in the authority of Scripture is not determined by cognitive constructs alone. Rather, it is greatly determined by the pentecostal's immediate experiences of God in, and through

> the text...pentecostal experience informs one's understanding of the text; yet the text *testifies* of the same experiences among the early church and the apostles.'[6]

Testimony is therefore an important constituent of the pentecostal and charismatic traditions.[7] While tradition may have a negative connotation, it is now widely accepted that we all do our theology from some kind of position or tradition, that is a linguistic-cultural context. Tradition, which is living, is open to change and transformation, but nevertheless provides a platform from which to speak, act and judge. Of course, with a living tradition, it merges into the contemporary and experiential side of faith and practice. It is here that testimony is perhaps most obvious.[8] The occasion for someone to testify to what God has done and is doing, within the context of worship, provides the key to understanding testimony in its cohering function of the other sources of Christian and general knowledge.

As Scripture is read and expounded , so God's testimony through the writings of his servants is heard

Pentecostal Testimony in Worship and Bible Study

R Jerome Boone—in an insightful article in which he considers the relationship between worship, community and pentecostal formation—outlines the components he would expect to see in a pentecostal service of worship.[9]

> These components are: (1) congregational singing, often functioning in a mode of celebration; (2) prayer, which is offered with the expectation of results associated with a clear belief in the supernatural; (3) testimony, through which the individual gives a personal account of their life in Christ; (4) sermon, which is a counterpart to the testimony and declares the story and vision of God; and (5) altar services, by which he means the opportunity to receive prayer ministry in response to the preached word.

In the context of a worshipping and witnessing community people are given the opportunity to interpret their stories of faith within the context of both the biblical story and the story of the particular community to which they belong. To appreciate the nature of testimony within the pentecostal tradition it is necessary to turn to another contemporary approach.

Jackie David Johns and Cheryl Bridges Johns have offered an important model for group Bible study.[10] They suggest an approach that is holistic in terms of knowledge of God. In this model knowledge of God is primarily through an encounter with him rather than abstract speculation. The Holy Spirit mediates this knowledge in the context of the community and by means of the Scriptures. Thus they suggest that the group begin the Bible study by sharing their testimony of life in the Spirit. This is followed by the activity of searching the Scriptures in an effort to know the word of God. The group is subsequently asked to yield to the Spirit, since the Spirit is the agent of encounter with the holy God resulting in transformation. Finally there is the response to the call to live in the Father's presence. Those who have yielded to the word of the Spirit in Scripture are convicted and transformed. Thus a new testimony emerges, 'one in which we confess what we have seen and what we have heard and what we are compelled to be and do.'[11] For our purposes it is worth outlining briefly what features of testimony these authors expect to be included.

In this model, people are encouraged to share of themselves through the delivery of personal testimony. Each and every person knows what it means to live in a fallen and sinful world. Thus the uncertainties of our life in Christ are not hidden. Individuals offer themselves to the group for shared critical reflection and thereby contribute to the corporate testimony of the group and community. Memory pulls the past into the present, and gives expression to 'feelings, values and understandings.'[12] Through the act of remembering the person engages in the process of reflection that both selects information and interprets it in the context in which the testimony is offered. It is something that is offered for the glory of God and for the edification of the body of Christ.

> *Testimony is offered for the glory of God and for the edification of the body of Christ*

As the group receives the testimony its members are encouraged to process their own memories and situations. The testimony is also shared in anticipation of the future, when the kingdom of God will be consummated. In dialogue with the Scriptures, the dissonance of living in the 'now but not yet' of God's reign is faced. The group leader facilitates this process by studying the passage herself beforehand, and by raising questions or issues which call for open discussion and full participation in the shared reflection.

There is a great deal that church leaders can learn from this model about enabling people to experience God in Word and Spirit. In terms of a public setting, there has been much testimony on the subject of the 'Toronto Blessing.'[13] However, it is worth considering the subject of testimony in the Bible before turning our attention to a specific testimony as an example of the role of testimony in worship.

3

Walter Brueggemann, in his Theology of the Old Testament, *uses the concept of testimony and the metaphor of trial as co-ordinating ideas through which to structure an approach to Old Testament study.*[14]

This reflects the importance of the concept in the Bible and therefore for Christian theology. In the Old Testament the notion of testimony is based upon an act of encounter between the person and God, to which the person gives testimony—for example Moses and the burning bush (Exodus 3).[15] This is also seen in Moses' encounter with Yahweh at Sinai. As a consequence, 'testimony' in the Pentateuch often refers to the decalogue or the tent of meeting (Exodus 29.4) or the ark of the covenant (Exodus 40.3). That is, these things function as evidence that calls to mind particular events of encounter between God and his people. This evidence becomes a basis of revelation in terms of the Torah. The idea of testimony is further developed in the sense of a legal setting through the Old Testament (see, for example, Numbers 35.50, Deuteronomy 19.15, 18). In the book of the prophet Isaiah (Isaiah 43.10, 12, 44.8) the nation of Israel is ordered to come forward as a witness to the other nations regarding the unique righteousness of Yahweh. The scene is one of bringing a case against the nations as a final judgement on the world.

Paul Ricoeur, in an important essay on the hermeneutics of testimony, comments on the Isaiah 43.8–13 passage:

> The irruption of meaning is fourfold. At first the witness is not just anyone who comes forward and gives testimony, but the one who is sent in order to testify. Originally, testimony comes from somewhere else. Next, the witness does not testify about isolated and contingent fact but about the radical, global meaning of human experience. It is Yahweh himself who is witnessed to in the testimony. Moreover, the testimony is orientated toward proclamation, divulging, propagation: it is for all peoples that one people witness. Finally, this profession implies a total engagement not only of words but of acts and, in the extreme, in the sacrifice of life. What separates this new meaning of

In the New Testament there is evidence of a legal framework within the Synoptic gospels (as in Mark 14.55, 56, 59; Luke 22.71); future legal testimony of the disciples is anticipated as public witness to Jesus in the hostile environment of persecution (Mark 10.18). Luke, in the Acts of the Apostles, uses the concept of testimony in the general sense of attestation to good conduct (Acts 16.2; 22.5, 12) or a good name (Acts 6.3) as well as in reference to false witnesses (Acts 6.13, 7.58). However, in Acts 23.11 the verb 'to bear witness' means to proclaim Christ and is associated with the apostolic testimony of the gospel (Acts 4.33).

> For Luke it is the apostles, the disciples, who have been commissioned by Jesus with the proclamation of the message of the kingdom, who are witnesses. They are more precisely defined in Acts 1.22 as witnesses of the resurrection of Jesus (cf Acts 2.32; 3.15; 13.31; 26.16—Paul, because the risen Lord met him) and of his deeds (also predicted in Acts 22.15 of Paul).[17]

For Paul too the concept of testimony usually refers to the proclamation of the gospel (1 Cor 1.6; 2.1; 2 Thess 1.10).

The concept of witness has a more central role in the Johannine material.[18] Although John in his gospel is aware of the classical sense of testimony as human attestation (John 2.25; 18.23; 12.17; 3.28; 8.17), testimony chiefly concerns testimony to or of Christ. Therefore, John the Baptist testifies to Jesus (1.7, 8, 15, 32; 3.26, 31). Jesus testifies to the truth concerning himself (John 8.13, 14—in tension with 5.31). He also states that his works (John 5.36, 10.25), his Father (5.32, 37; 6.65) and the Scriptures (5.39) all bear witness to him. Jesus himself witnesses to the truth (John 18.37) because of what he has known and seen (John 3.11). In John's gospel, therefore, Jesus, like Moses, is a mediator of the testimony or revelation of God to the world (John 3.31–34; 7.16; 12.48–50). The world rejects his testimony (John 8.14) and is judged by the witness who is also the judge.

In John's gospel Jesus is a mediator of the testimony or revelation of God to the world

The Johannine material also contains references to the confirmation of God's truth through the testimony of believers. Thus, the Samaritans believe in Jesus on account of the Samaritan woman encountered by Jesus at the well (John 4.29). In addition to the witness of the Spirit of truth, the Paraclete

(John 15.26), the disciples of Jesus are also expected to testify to Jesus (John 15.27). The epistles especially stress the role of testimony in the proclamation of the gospel (1 John 1.2; 4.14). This is again witnessed to by the Spirit (1 John 5.6) and is carried by the believer (1 John 5.10). Thus testimony is something which is experienced by faith and known through faith in the context of a believing community.

This is stated well by Andrew T Lincoln in the context of the lawsuit motif in John's gospel:

> Just as Jesus' witness to truth is self-authenticating, so the community's witness to Jesus in its written testimony is self-authenticating. In an inevitable circularity, the community claims that its own witness is true. In the end, in knowing where truth lies in the cosmic lawsuit, there can be no going behind the witness. This would be to assume that there is some superior vantage point from which to make a judgment; if, as the narrative claims, the truth of the lawsuit is about God, then by definition there can be no such vantage point. In line with such a perspective, the response the narrative calls for is acceptance of its witness or belief. The only way to discover its truth for oneself, to align oneself with true judgment in the world, is to participate in it by believing. Hence Jesus' words to Pilate, 'Everyone who belongs to the truth listens to my voice' (18.37). The attitude that correlates to this narrative's notion of truth is faith seeking understanding, or as Jesus puts it earlier: 'Anyone who resolves to do the will of God will know whether the teaching is from God or whether I am speaking on my own' (7.17) and 'believe...so that you may know and understand that the Father is in me and I am in the Father' (10.38).[19]

The Revelation of John refers to the testimony of Jesus Christ as the word of God (Revelation 1.2, 9; 12.11). Testimony of Jesus is the 'spirit of prophecy' (19.10). To be touched by the testimony of Jesus Christ places the recipient in the service of the witness. This also means sharing in the persecution and suffering of Christ (Revelation 12.11). Since Jesus is the faithful witness *par excellence* (Revelation 1.5) it is anticipated that those in Christ will also be faithful witnesses to the gospel (Revelation 2.13) and hold firmly to the hope that is set before them.

Testimony as Speech Act 4

C A J Coady considers testimony to be a speech act performed under certain conditions and with certain intentions.[20]

The contexts for such speech acts are defined in terms of the formal setting, the informal context and the extended sense.[21] By *formal testimony*, he refers to the kind of testimony that is offered in a court of law, commission or enquiry that is provided by persons who are regarded as witnesses. *Informal testimony* refers to the natural testimony of everyday life. It includes such things as giving geographical directions, reporting an incident that has happened, and giving a football score. *Extended testimony* refers to the practice of reporting information based on sources other than firsthand experience. For example, historians refer to documents such as private diaries, confidential minutes of meetings and newspaper reports as testimony. In a church context, formal testimony would correspond to the kind used in a worship service when a leader interviews someone or creates space for testimony from the congregation. Informal testimony happens within casual conversation especially in the small group settings. Extended testimony can be found in popular magazines or church newsletters and bulletins. In order to appreciate the nature of formal testimony, which can be seen for example in the formal testimonies produced by churches and Christian organizations, it is useful to note the characteristics set out by Coady. He defines the marks of formal testimony in the following way:

(a) it is a form of evidence;

(b) it is constituted by person A offering their remarks *as* evidence so that we are invited to accept p because A says p;[22]

(c) the person offering the remarks is in a position to do so—he or she has the relevant authority, competence, or credentials;

(d) the testifier has been given a certain status in the enquiry by being formally acknowledged as a witness and by giving his evidence with due ceremony;

(e) as a specification of (c) within English law and proceedings influenced by it, the testimony is normally required to be firsthand (*ie* not hearsay);

(f) as a corollary of (a) the testifier's remarks should be relevant to a

> disputed or unresolved question and should be directed to those who are in need of evidence on the matter.[23]

He proposes that some of these characteristics can be found within natural testimony (a, b, and f), although other characteristics are less obvious (c, d, and e). Most of the reports accepted as testimony are not firsthand; there is much less scepticism towards hearsay in this context (as indeed is the case of formal legal testimony within Scottish and much Continental law).[24] The different context of natural testimony means that it should be considered more akin to promising than giving evidence. There is acceptance of a clear connection between how a person says things are with how they actually are.[25] Having said that, natural testimony is often believed because of the relevant competence, authority or credentials of the person testifying, even though such credentials are not formalized in an institutional manner.

Coady argues that fundamentally we believe the testimony of an individual because we trust the witness. The witness has a particular kind of authority to speak on the matter in question. The attitude of trust is fundamental but not blind.

> What happens characteristically in the reception of testimony is that the audience operates a sort of learning mechanism which has certain critical capacities built into it. The mechanism may be thought of as partly innate, though modified by experience, especially in the matter of critical capacities. It is useful to invoke the model of a mechanism here since the reception of testimony is normally unreflective but it is not thereby uncritical. We may have 'no reason to doubt' another's communication even where there is no question of our being gullible; we may simply recognize that the standard warning signs of deceit, confusion, or mistake are not present.[26]

He suggests that we naturally begin with an inevitable commitment to some degree of reliability.[27] This is enforced when we find cohesion and coherence with our expectations. It is here that local and cultural factors play their part in determining what is and what is not believable. Indeed, 'we require a conceptual apparatus and related beliefs in order to construe our experience at all.'[28] When this is related to pentecostal and charismatic understanding of knowledge we can see that the testimony of Scripture as reliable and its ongoing narrative power to form the cultural-linguistic context provide the crucial matrix from within which to benefit from and appreciate the role of testimony. As we have seen, in Scripture we find that testimony is a central feature as the biblical writers give testimony to God's purposes through the two testaments of Old and New.

A Case Study: Terry's Testimony 5

In 1995 I was able to visit the Toronto Airport Vineyard Church, as it was called then.

It was later to be named the Toronto Airport Christian Fellowship (TACF), following a breach with John Wimber and the Vineyard Church leadership.[29] During my visit I experienced what some people came to call the 'Toronto Blessing,'[30] and purchased a couple of teaching video tapes which illustrate some of the testimonies given by visitors to the church.

In the video entitled *Decently and in Order*[31] the first testimony recorded during a service is delivered by an Australian named 'Terry.' This testimony would normally be delivered after a period of worship through songs led by a worship leader and musicians. Testimonies are delivered just prior to the sermon. The sermon is then followed by an invitation to receive prayer ministry. The video material is introduced by the Senior Pastor of the church, John Arnott. He explains that this material contains the testimony and experience of people who have been powerfully touched and blessed by the Holy Spirit who has transformed their lives. The manifestations are indications of the work of the Holy Spirit as he affects lives and bears fruit. In this narrative the key words are testimony, experience, power, transformation, Holy Spirit and fruit.

Terry is an Australian who is bursting to tell what God has done in his life. He is the Senior Pastor of a church in Sydney. In response to the invitation by John Arnott to tell what has happened, he recalls how back in Australia he was dissatisfied with his Christian life and the life of the church. For months and months, he had been seeking God, when he read in the *Charisma* magazine what was happening in Toronto. He attempted to contact Arnott but failed—so he boarded a plane! As soon as he arrived he sensed God beginning to work upon him. Things that he did not want to do, such as cry, he found himself doing. As the Holy Spirit encountered him, God showed him things about his life.

He explained that he was put into an orphanage at the age of two years old. During his pastoral ministry he could not understand people's pain and so when they came for counselling he would dismiss them quickly. It was not until he arrived at the Toronto church and experienced the touch of the Spirit that he experienced his own pain. In this time, God had shown Terry to himself as a little child and reminded him about his father. He met his father for the first time thirty years after being in the orphanage. Indeed, the Spirit reminded him that his father was, ironically, a French Canadian. The consequence of this revelation is that he has been set free, liberated. He is a new man. He now understands what pain children experience because he had just experienced it himself. He had closed it off for nearly forty years. That was why he could not understand the pain of others.

John Arnott interpreted this experience as a vision from the Holy Spirit to Terry's heart. He explains to the congregation present that the fruit of the Spirit's work is so good. Admittedly, the manifestations of the Spirit do not make a lot of sense to the natural mind. It is impossible without this story to understand why such a man might cry out in such pain. However, once you understand his story of rejection and his pain, then it begins to make sense. Indeed, he argues that you simply cannot evaluate the works of the heart by watching the phenomena that people go through when the power of the Holy Spirit comes upon them. It will take newcomers to the church a few days, therefore, to process what is happening here. His advice is to 'go with the flow' for a while. The test is the fruit that is produced.

He interpreted this experience as a vision from the Holy Spirit to Terry's heart

Arnott continues by emphasizing that what he is talking about are lives that have been transformed, that have had 'heart transplants' and who are more in love with Jesus than they ever were before. That kind of 'fruit' is not deception. He asks the congregation: Which spirit produces greater love for Jesus? They answer emphatically: the Holy Spirit. He agrees and says that it is very biblical for lives to be transformed. Jesus said that he had come to bind up the broken hearted, set the captives free and preach the acceptable year of the Lord, the year of Jubilee. He suggests to Terry that his heart has only realized just how much the Lord loves him. His head may have known it for years but that it did not 'get into' the total man. He does not understand why Christians have been told to deny their emotions—it is part of the whole person.

John Arnott concludes this interview in front of the congregation by asking Terry if he can pray for him. At that moment a number of the ministry team gather around Terry, including John's wife, Carol. They pray for him and Terry falls forward under the power of the Spirit. Arnott then proceeds to preach to the congregation regarding the manifestations of the Spirit. At a point early in the sermon, Terry groans out aloud, to some hilarity from the congregation. Arnott interprets this with humour as clearly the congrega-

tion are amused. He concludes by adding that the reason Terry is groaning is
because there is 'power going through him.'

Analysis and Reflection on Terry's Testimony

I want to suggest that the category of testimony is a fundamental category
within human knowledge in general but that it takes on supreme importance within the spirituality of the pentecostal and charismatic traditions.

It functions as a social integrating centre for the other sources of human
knowledge, including knowledge of God mediated by revelation. In an at-
tempt to transpose Coady's model in terms of Terry's testimony the following
observations can be made (the letters refer back to the outline on page 11).

The context of the testimony presents itself in terms of evidence (a). The
'Toronto Blessing' was and is controversial. As a consequence of the attention the church in Toronto received from visitors and the media, as well as
theological concerns, John Wimber removed himself from pastoral oversight.
In effect he excommunicated the church from the Vineyard denomination.
Consequently, the church aims to present evidence in the form of audio-
video material to explain what God is doing. In the context of the service,
the testimony provides evidence of what is happening to the person when
experiencing certain physical phenomena. The visitor or enquirer is told by
Arnott that it will take some time to process what is happening. Thus the
evidence of the testimony is relevant to the audience, broadens the horizon
of understanding and prepares the individual to receive a blessing from God
(f). When the interview is followed by further prayer ministry, the phenomena are demonstrated again. The testimony is further ratified as coherent, at
least in terms of its relation to phenomena.

We are invited to accept Terry's testimony as evidence because of his recent
and ongoing experience of God demonstrated by the phenomena (b). The
story and the phenomena that follow the interview demonstrate its firsthand
nature (e). We are also invited to accept his testimony because of who he is.
He is the Senior Pastor of a big church in Sydney, Australia. He therefore
has, within the Vineyard church tradition, the relevant authority, competence and credentials to be trusted (c). He is a reliable and credible witness.[32]

The central figure in the church, John Arnott, has given Terry a certain status
in that particular meeting by inviting him to testify in public (d). Clearly his
story had been ascertained and approved for delivery in public, just as any
competent lawyer would assess the quality of a legal witness.[33] This status
was given due ceremony by locating it in a central place in the service, just
before the sermon, and by following the testimony with prayer again. Thus
the testimony is located within the ceremony of liturgy—it has a clearly

defined place in the order. It is also followed by the charismatically understood ritual of 'falling over,' or being 'slain in the Spirit.'

Clearly this testimony is given with an interpretive framework provided by the Toronto Airport Christian Fellowship. This framework is provided largely by the Vineyard model, which promotes charismatic evangelicalism. John Arnott's introduction of the material within the video already sets the interpretive framework within which visitors and viewers encounter what is happening. His careful interpretation of what Terry is saying adds value to the testimony material and helps the congregation appreciate the significance of the *divine-human encounter* in Terry's life.

This testimony is located within the ceremony of liturgy

Terry's perceptions and experience were to some extent shaped by his personal history of rejection and spiritual dryness. His desire and search for God was demonstrated in his reading about the 'Toronto Blessing' in the *Charisma* magazine. Thus the testimony of the revival is distributed via the wider media structures of the charismatic movement and prepared him for what he was able to meet in Toronto. The testimony remains silent with regard to his memory of God's previous encounters with him, but his memory of the pain of rejection as a child is significant to the nature of the testimony.

The use of Scripture and the ministry of Jesus gives *legitimation* to what happens in the church. There is a direct correspondence drawn between what Jesus did in the life of people as witnessed to in Scripture and what he does in the lives of people today. The loose quotation of Luke 4.18–19 (Isaiah 61.1–2) by John Arnott illustrates the need to connect Terry's experience to the ministry of Jesus in the gospels.

The language of *transformation* is obvious and significant. Terry came to Toronto because he wanted to be changed. He had been changed and was continuing to be ministered to (clearly his time at the church had not yet drawn to a close). He demonstrated an experiential understanding of knowledge; he expected to know God as a God of transformation. In this testimony, there is a clear 'carry over of value' as the love of God is realized in terms of a renewed love within Terry himself. This is a direct result of the *encounter* with the Spirit of God. Terry's sense of rejection and his inability to sense people's pain is healed by the love of God. As a consequence, he anticipates that he would be able to love his own child and his congregation more on his return. This is change indeed, a first fruit of the kingdom of God! But the long-term transformation of Terry is of primary importance and we are unable to assess this except by further work. Therefore all such endorsement from this vantage point should be of a preliminary kind.

Theological & Practical Guidelines 6

In order to promote and encourage the use of testimony in worship and in Christian discipleship, a number of guidelines can be suggested.

However, these guidelines are merely that—they represent my thoughts on the issues surrounding the practical use of testimony in groups. They are suggestions rather than prescriptive assertions.

1. Building Awareness

If your church does not have opportunities for people to share testimonies in the worship context, then it probably means that you will have to raise awareness of the importance of testimony. People can be very sensitive to this area, feeling that individuals are making a bid for power. Therefore, it is wise to start small. I would suggest that testimony should be introduced in the small group setting initially. In the house group or mid-week prayer meeting, the role of testimony can be explained and people encouraged to share their stories very naturally with one another. It may be that the group leader can arrange for group exercises to occur, such as sharing stories in pairs before one or two give a testimony to the larger group. It is important at the early stages that people feel affirmed and encouraged rather than criticized because they do not have the right 'Christian' or 'church' language. This is more like the natural testimony which Coady mentions.

2. Nurturing Trust

If you wish to appropriate testimony in the more formal setting of the worship service, you face a dilemma. The need to offer a structure through which you encourage testimony will, of necessity, constrain it. If you promote spontaneous testimonies from the congregation, this may only work well in a relatively small group where everyone can hear what is said and feel sufficiently confident to participate. In a larger congregational setting, the people testifying to God's grace will need to use a microphone and therefore have access to the leadership 'space' at the front of the service. Here, where additional authority can be assumed by those using 'official' leadership space, it is important to have some kind of discernment process. An inappropriate message at an inopportune time can be disastrous for congregational worship, and from which a congregation make take quite a time to recover. Anticipated negative effects should be guarded against. The key to good testimony is trust. Initially you may have to work hard to built up trust, since initial and natural credulity to others may have been damaged. Therefore testimony needs careful nurture and discernment if it is to become an acceptable and normal part of weekly worship.

The key to good testimony is trust

3. Developing Accountability

Every person, including the clergy, who wishes to testify to God's grace operating in their life should be accountable to others. It is important that someone in the meeting or service takes responsibility for the discernment of testimony, as for prophecy. Failure to do so could lead to abuse of power and manipulation. In a sense, then, the giving of a testimony has some resemblance to the giving of a prophecy, except that it is encoded within a personal narrative and does not claim the same degree of divine authority. Nevertheless, the principle of accountability is important and needs to be recognized and affirmed.

4. Monitoring Delivery

The delivery of testimony can be exciting, mediocre or dreary, depending upon the person. Testimonies in a formal setting are not going to work unless they are delivered well. I do not mean that people need to have polished spoken English—few of us would preach if that were the case! But it does mean that styles of delivery can be encouraged which are straight-to-the-point and easily followed by the congregation. The testimony, in my opinion, should contain sufficient content to make it a testimony—in other words there has to be sufficient narrative and information to make it interesting. It should be put in a context; the person may not be known by newcomers or visitors to the church so a sentence of personal introduction helps, as does the context of the story itself. The testimony should also be relevant and up-to-date. What is the point of the testimony? What does it actually say about life in the kingdom of God? A good structure which describes the process of charismatic spirituality is: search; encounter; and transformation. These words encapsulate Terry's testimony and also provide a coherent structure for the testimony itself.

A helpful structure is search; encounter; an transformation

5. Conducting Interviews

Testimonies can be achieved in the formal setting by means of an interview. This can be an excellent way of drawing out the value of a testimony, especially in a large group setting. However, the person conducting the interview needs to be skilful in both allowing the person to testify and interpreting the story in a way that is affirming and positive. It is certainly not the place for an argument or disagreement! If interviewers are to be used, I would suggest that they should be trained in interview techniques. They should be especially aware of the possibilities for the manipulation of the story by them as well as the way in which a good interview technique can enrich the testimony.

6. Connecting with Reality

Testimonies should also reflect the realities of life here on planet Earth! They should not be filled with 'pie in the sky when I die,' although a healthy end-time orientation is important. After all, the Christian life continues beyond death and resurrection hope is an important feature of biblically informed discipleship now. Once this is said, though, the importance of God's in-breaking rule now is brought into focus—God does act to save, heal and restore broken relationships. But his absence, or perceived absence must also be noted as a hidden presence. Too many pentecostal testimonies are banal and simply a repetition of catch-phrases, normally around being saved, sanctified and filled with the Holy Ghost! However, as Scott A Ellington has noted, the Bible also contains testimonies of lament.[34] He argues that the loss of testimony in the community's life is also a loss of lament, for which we are the poorer. He argues for a greater honesty in what we testify to, including elements of lament. Pastorally, of course, this can become a difficult area but if managed well it can become a blessing because honesty will also flow into other people's lives. It also means that when there is a testimony of God's goodness and changed lives the possibility for a greater integrity is present because of the opportunity for critique through the presence of lament. In this way an unrealistically euphoric approach to testimony can be avoided.

We need a greater honesty in what we testify to, including elements of lament

7. Using Opportunities

There are all sorts of opportunities for creating space for testimony. Historically, the pentecostals have been very good at this and there are now archives in various countries with testimony material reaching back to the Azusa Street revival of 1906. The charismatic renewal movement does not have the same historical awareness, nor the interest and funding to support such endeavours. Nevertheless, charismatics can encourage the use of the category of extended testimony through parish magazines and church bulletins. Where the church has a website, it could be interesting to publish a testimony or two and see what interest is generated as an experiment in evangelism. It would also be good for testimonies to be catalogued and kept by churches so that they can be reviewed periodically by the leadership to see in what way God has moved in people's lives. If this is done, it will also mean that a future generation of researchers will have a rich source of material with which to work.

8. Discerning Prayerfully

Finally, within charismatic spirituality with its accent on prayer, all testimony should be considered, initially by the person testifying and subsequently by the congregation or group, within the context of prayer. The purpose of testimony is the same as other gifts of the Spirit, namely the edification of the body of Christ. Whilst it may contain challenge and be highly personalized stylistically (testimonies are highly subjective and prone to being ego-centric), nevertheless its purpose is not self-serving but God-serving and church-serving. Therefore, the attitude of the person testifying must include at its heart humility as well as honesty. But these attitudes are primarily attitudes before God. Pentecostals stress the nature of knowledge in terms of the affections—we love God with all our hearts not just our minds. Testimony arises from a relationship of love between the person and the triune God. It also expresses itself in love for one's neighbour. Such an attitude will seek above all else the glorification of the triune God. That is the ultimate motivation in giving one's testimony. In the process, one becomes vulnerable and that vulnerability needs to be recognized as a place of encounter with the divine. Therefore, the Holy Spirit invites participation in this relational dynamic, so that other people may also be drawn into the divine life and participate in the life that is God's.

Vulnerability needs to be recognized as a place of encounter with the divine

Testimony and the Liturgy 7

The Church of England's life and tradition as expressed through its liturgy has never been open to the role of testimony—until the arrival of Common Worship.

The new liturgy in the Church of England has an openness and flexibility to an extent not seen before. It is in the context of the new Baptism and Confirmation services that we are able to appreciate that a role for testimony has been found—albeit a small one! For the purposes of this discussion, I shall focus on the confirmation service (although recognizing the baptism service in this respect is similar). The structure of the Confirmation service can be summarized in this way:

Preparation: greeting
                     hymn
                     collect

Liturgy of the Word: Scripture readings
                     sermon

Liturgy of Initiation: presentation of the candidates[35]
                     (testimony by the candidates)
                     decision
                     profession of faith
                     confirmation (with invoking of the Spirit)
                     commission
                     prayers of intercession
                     peace

Liturgy of the Eucharist follows

During the presentation of the candidates the bishop asks them: Have you been baptized in the name of the Father, and of the Son, and of the Holy Spirit? Each one replies: I have. He then asks: Are you ready with your own mouth and from your own heart to affirm your faith in Jesus Christ? Each one replies: I am. It is at this point that testimonies from the candidates *may* follow. Liturgically, it is an option and not mandatory. However, this means that the opportunity for such an occasion provided for testimony will in the majority of occasions not be used. Some bishops, unsure of the quality of the testimonies, may in fact never allow the use of this option.

From a charismatic perspective it is interesting to observe that the actual confirmation section of the service contains two prayers concerned with the Spirit which candidates could find even more edifying and spiritually significant if they followed a personal testimony. First the bishop prays:

> Almighty and ever-living God,
> You have given these your servants new birth
> in baptism by water and the Spirit,
> and have forgiven them all their sins.
> Let your Holy Spirit rest upon them:
> the Spirit of wisdom and understanding;
> the Spirit of counsel and inward strength;
> the Spirit of knowledge and true godliness;
> and let their delight be in the fear of the Lord. Amen.

The bishop then affirms the candidates' calling by God and asks the Lord to confirm them with the Holy Spirit. After this the bishop invites the congregation to pray for all those on whom hands have been laid with the prayer:

> Defend, O Lord, these your servants with your heavenly grace,
> that they may continue yours for ever,
> and daily increase in your Holy Spirit more and more
> until they come to your everlasting kingdom. Amen.

The bishop subsequently follows this prayer with a commission of the candidates to walk in the way of Jesus Christ.

It is disappointing to observe that while testimony is included, it is regarded as an optional extra. Here is a wonderful occasion to affirm the candidate's story intertwined within God's story of salvation. The Holy Spirit has drawn the person into divine fellowship with the triune God and this is an exciting opportunity for such a witness to be made with their own mouth and from their own heart. A recent commentary on the new rite of Confirmation pays but a cursory glance towards testimony but not much more.[36] However, the commentary by Gilly Myers is much more helpful. She principally locates her advice concerning testimony in relation to the Baptism service but it could equally apply to both Baptism and Confirmation services. She even suggests a testimony rehearsal for large services including practise at using the microphone—sound advice in every sense of the word![37]

However, I would like to suggest that the Confirmation service provides a liturgical possibility for testimony that can be used within other liturgical forms of *Common Worship*. Firstly, in the Confirmation service the bishop seeks to discern that the candidates wish to testify with their own mouth and from their own heart regarding their life in Christ. The invitation: 'Is there anyone here ready to testify with their own mouth and from their own heart to their faith in Jesus Christ?' could be an important liturgical invitation and signal for use generally.

Secondly, after the testimony some members of the congregation, together with the minister, could gather around the person in charismatic style, and laying hands upon them, pray that the Holy Spirit would indeed anoint them afresh and empower them for continued service in Christ. In this way both the prayer of bishop and the congregational prayer would be joined together to indicate that the in-filling of the Holy Spirit in the life of the believer is a dynamic and ongoing process. It affirms that the Spirit is given *primarily* to the whole people of God rather than ecclesiastical hierarchies!

This liturgical structure and opportunity could then be used flexibly within *A Service of the Word*:[38]

Preparation
    greeting
    confession
    collect

Liturgy of the Word
    proclaim and respond to the word of God

Prayers
    pray for the church and the world

Liturgy of the Sacrament/Conclusion

The opportunity to respond to the word of God surely includes the possibility for the delivery of testimonies. Such testimonies could very naturally be used either to begin a service or to facilitate the transition from liturgy of the word to prayer for the church and the world.

In addition, the service for *A Celebration of Wholeness and Healing* also provides another context for testimony. Charismatic Christians expect God to heal people. This service puts the accent on prayer for people within a very structured context:[39]

Gathering
> greeting
> dialogue
> collect

Liturgy of the Word
> readings and psalm
> Gospel reading
> sermon

Prayers and Penitence
> [introduction]
> intercession
> penitence

Laying on of Hands and Anointing
> prayer over the oil
> laying on of hands
> [anointing]
> the Lord's prayer

[Liturgy of the Sacrament]

The Sending Out
> proclamation
> [the peace]
> [blessing]
> dismissal

For testimony to be used in this setting effectively it would have to function in a regular way. Therefore, testimonies resulting from *previous* healing services would be offered in the actual service. They could be offered either in the liturgy of the word or after the prayers for penitence but would definitely need to precede the laying on of hands (and anointing with oil).

It seems strange that Anglicanism wishes to restrict testimony to moments of spiritual crisis (Baptism and Confirmation). It is, of course, entirely appropriate that testimony be offered at these important points on the journey. However, to limit testimony to these points is to miss out on a vital opportunity to empower the people of God with his story as the Holy Spirit is ministering and working through them for the sake of his Kingdom. There are real lessons to be learnt from the informal liturgies of pentecostals and charismatic Christians in this regard. It is a pity that very few Anglican liturgists, if any, have done serious work in this direction.

Conclusion

8

The notion of testimony is basic to the biblical revelation. Indeed, the personal encounter of God with Moses provides the backdrop to the language of testimony in the Old Testament.

The forensic language of testimony continues throughout the Bible. The New Testament makes clear that testimony of encounter with God is inextricably tied to the person of Jesus Christ—his life and ministry, death and resurrection, especially his resurrection. All testimony, if it is to continue in this respect, should have a Christological focus. Terry's testimony talks of the Father's love and thus puts the Christology within a Trinitarian frame of reference. This is what Jesus does with respect to his own testimony. He testifies on behalf of the Father and says that the Paraclete will continue to testify about him after he has returned to the Father (John 14–16). Given the concern of pentecostals and charismatics to integrate their knowledge of God by means of community testimony, the biblical survey demonstrates just what a sound basis they have chosen. John's gospel states that the Paraclete will help the disciples in the testifying to the truth of encounter (John 15.26–27). Yet the biblical material, especially in John's gospel, also indicates that such testimony is discerned spiritually through the eyes of faith. The testimony of the faithful will be rejected by the world, as then, so now. So long as pentecostals and charismatics continue to keep the person and work of Jesus Christ within Christological and Trinitarian paradigms as the standard by which they judge such testimonies, then testimonies can continue to be regarded as authentically Christian. Therefore the testimony of Scripture as the supreme witness to the purposes of God in Christ functions in a critical way even as the testimony of the church as community functions in a cohering way.

> *Testimony of encounter with God is inextricablyy tied to the person of Jesus Christ*

> *The testimony of the faithful will be rejected by the world, as then, so now*

If the role of testimony within pentecostal and charismatic theology is so significant, why is there a limited role for it within Anglican churches involved in renewal? Of course, we give testimony in an informal and natural way all the time—we simply tell our stories. That is how it should be. But where in the communal and liturgical life of our churches is there space to hear and respond to testimony from our brothers and sisters in Christ? I have made some suggestions in this regard. Our structures need to be more flexible in order to affirm and appreciate this social dimension of knowledge that God has given us. Furthermore, perhaps the ecclesiastical culture of Anglicanism needs to be 'opened out' in order to appreciate more fully the transforming power of God as experienced in the lives of people. In this regard the role of testimony in worship is a significantly neglected feature of charismatic spirituality. It therefore invites further informed and sustained theological attention and liturgical development.

Why is there a limited role for testimony within Anglican churches involved in renewal?

Notes

1   Some of this material has been previously published in M Cartledge, 'The Role of Testimony in Worship,' *Anglicans for Renewal—Skepsis* 87 (2001) pp 27–31.

2   A E McGrath, *Christian Spirituality* (Oxford: Blackwell, 1999) p 2.

3   See M A McIntosh, *Mystical Theology* (Oxford: Blackwell, 1998) pp 3–34.

4   R Audi, *Epistemology: A Contemporary Introduction to the Theory of Knowledge* (London: Routledge, 1998, 2000) p 318.

5   Audi, *Epistemology*, p 320.

6   P W Lewis, 'Towards a Pentecostal Epistemology: The Role of Experience in Pentecostal Hermeneutics,' *The Spirit & Church* 2.1 (2000) pp 95–125 (pp 110–111, my emphasis); and S A Ellington, 'History, Story, and Testimony: Locating Truth in a Pentecostal Hermeneutic,' *PNEUMA: The Journal of the Society for Pentecostal Studies* 23.2 (2001) pp 245–263 (p 245), who gives the Bible a functional and absolute authority because of inspiration but maintains that for pentecostals biblical truth claims are *both* conceptual *and* experiential.

7   K J Archer, 'Pentecostal Hermeneutics: Retrospect and Prospect,' *Journal of Pentecostal Theology* 8 (1996) pp 63–81, suggests that this testimony can be encapsulated by the idea that God is breaking into the everyday lives of believers (p 69).

8   Lewis, 'Towards a Pentecostal Epistemology' p 99.

9   R J Boone, 'Community and Worship: The Key Components of Pentecostal Christian Formation,' *Journal of Pentecostal Theology* 8 (1996) pp 129–142.

10 J D Johns and C B Johns, 'Yielding to the Spirit: A Pentecostal Approach to Group Bible Study,' *Journal of Pentecostal Theology* 1 (1992) pp 109–134.

11 Johns and Johns, 'Yielding to the Spirit' p 134.

12 Johns and Johns, 'Yielding to the Spirit' p 126.

13 See, for example, the collection of testimonies in J Arnott, *Experience the Blessing: Testimonies from Toronto* (Ventura CA: Renew Books, 2000).

14 W Brueggemann, *Theology of the Old Testament: Testimony, Dispute, Advocacy* (Minneapolis: Fortress, 1997).

15 L Coenen, 'Witness,' in C Brown (ed), *The New International Dictionary of the New Testament*, Vol 3 (Exeter: Paternoster, 1978) pp 1038–1047.

16 P Ricoeur, 'The Hermeneutics of Testimony,' in P Ricoeur, *Essays on Biblical Interpretation* (London: SPCK, 1981) pp 119–154 (p 131).

17 Coenen, 'Witness' p 1044.

18 A T Lincoln, *Truth on Trial: The Lawsuit Motif in the Fourth Gospel* (Peabody, MA: Hendrickson, 2000) explains how the lawsuit motif contains the major themes of witness, interrogation, trial and judgment, *passim*.

19 Lincoln, *Truth on Trial*, p 230.

20 C A J Coady, *Testimony: A Philosophical Study* (Oxford: Clarendon Press, 1992, 2000) p 25.

21 Coady, *Testimony*, pp 27–53.

22 The denotation *p* refers to a given proposition.

23 Coady, *Testimony*, p 33.

24 Coady, *Testimony*, p 39.

25 Coady, *Testimony*, p 43.

26 Coady, *Testimony*, p 47.

27 This is reversed by D Middlemiss, *Interpreting Charismatic Experience* (London: SCM, 1996) who posits an initial approach of incredulity; see my review of his book in *Evangelical Quarterly* 71.1 (1999) pp 85–88.

28 Coady, *Testimony*, p 196.

29 For a brief account of the history and emphases of the Vineyard Churches, see Daniel E Albrecht, *Rites in the Spirit: A Ritual Approach to Pentecostal/Charismatic Spirituality* (Sheffield: Sheffield Academic Press, JPTS 17, 1999) pp 60–70.

30 My own account is recalled, with theological reflection, in Mark J Cartledge, 'A Spur to Holistic Discipleship' in David Hilborn (ed), *'Toronto' in Perspective: Papers on the New Charismatic Wave of the 1990s* (Carlisle: Evangelical Alliance / Paternoster, 2001) pp 64–71.

31 John Arnott, *Decently and in Order* (Toronto Airport Vineyard, 272 Attwell Drive, Toronto, Ontario, Canada, M9W 6M3, 1995).

32 For a collection of testimonies, see J Arnott (ed), *Experience the Blessing: Testimonies from Toronto* (Ventura, CA: Renew, Gospel Light, 2000)

33 S A Ellington, 'The Costly Loss of Testimony,' *Journal of Pentecostal Theology* 16 (2000) pp 48–59, following the work of M Poloma, notes how this control from the pulpit is a form of institutionalization (p 53). What could be suggested here is that it is congruent with a move from informal to more formal modes of testimony.

34 Ellington 'The Costly Loss of Testimony' p 53.

35 The Baptism service also allows within the presentation of the candidates that 'Testimony by the candidate(s) may follow,' see: 'The Liturgy of Baptism,' *Common Worship* (London: Church House Publishing, ©The Archbishops' Council 2000) p 352.

36 S Jones and P Tovey, 'Initiation Services' in P Bradshaw (ed), *Companion to Common Worship: Volume 1* (London: SPCK, 2001) p 174.

37 G Myers, *Initiation: Using Common Worship—A Practical Guide to the New Services* (London: Church House Publishing and Praxis, 2000) pp 30–31; see also M Earey and G Myers, *Common Worship Today: An Illustrated Guide to Common Worship* (London: HarperCollins, 2001) p 128.

38 *Common Worship*, p 25.

39 *Common Worship: Pastoral Services* (London: Church House Publishing, © The Archbishops' Council, 2000) p 13.